Circular Knitting Machine Patterns

Basic Circular Knitting Machine Patterns For Beginners

Copyright © 2023

DEDICATION

Contents

DIY Headband

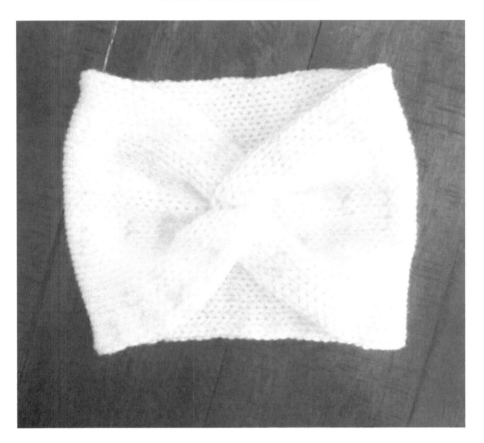

Addi-Express Kingsize (46 needle)

Baby Bee Sweet Delight yarn from Hobby Lobby

Yarn Materials:

Needle

Scissors

Crochet Hook 5mm

Step-By-Step Instructions

This tutorial does not teach the basics of using the Addi-Expess Kingsize

Step 1:

Cast On with Waste Yarn leaving a 6"-8" tail.

Crank out 5-10 rows.

Step 2: Color Change

Now take your project yarn and place a 24-36" tail in the center of your Addi.

Place yarn inside the gold yarn feeder and crank out the amount of rows according to size.

Circular Knitting Machine Patterns

Newborn: 60-65 rows

Toddler: 12-18 months 75 rows

Adult: 90 rows

Step 3: Color Change back to Waste Yarn

Cut a 24-36in. tail of your project yarn and color change to waste yarn.

Place waste yarn inside gold yarn feeder and crank out 5-10 rows.

Step 4: Cast Off

Cut yarn and throw tail in the center of your Addi.

Crank out 2 rows without yarn. Your tube will fall off the needles.

Step 5: Closing Yarn Tube

Sew each end closed using your 5mm crochet hook.

Single crochet a total of 23 times to close your tube. 23 times ensures you did not miss stitches.

Start with the first loop and the last loop to close your tube

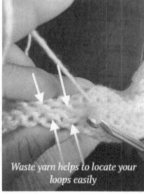

Waste yarn helps to locate your loops easily

You should have an equal number of loops at the end

Step 6: Sewing the "x"

Grab each end and pinch them together.

Slide them halfway together in an alternating pattern. Sew ends together.

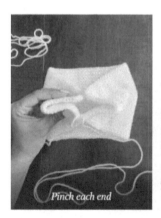

Pinch each end

Only sandwich the ends halfway leaving a hole on each end.

Sew together. Make sure to go through all 4 sections

Take the open holes and fold them over the part you just sewed together and sew these ends together.

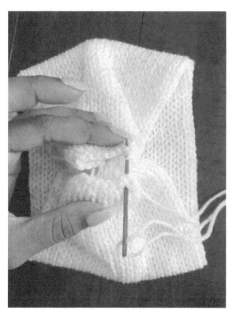 

Step 7:

Hide your tails within your headband by inserting your yarn needle through the first layer of your headband.

Congratulations, you just made an "x" closure headband!

Loom Knit Holiday Bag

Materials:

40 Pin and 46/48 Pin Knitting Machine

Worsted Weight Yarn:

Suggested yarns

Yarn for lining bag – Lion Brand Pound of Love

Yarn for outside of bag – Lion Brand Fisherman's Wool

US Size 7 Circular Knitting Needle used for casting off machine, though other methods of casting off will work

Ribbon

Darning Needle

Scissors

Tension: Tight (first hole only)

Other supplies:

Row Counter

Sizes:

Size will vary depending on how many rows you do and on what machine you use. About 4 rounds is roughly 1 inch of fabric.

Gauge: 2" x 2" is 8 stitches x 8 rows

Start with waste yarn and cast on and crank out 10 rounds or so.

Switch to Yarn for the lining and crank out 45 rounds

Loosely tie on main color yarn and crank out 65 rounds for a total of 110 Rounds.

Cast off by using one of the circular knitting needles, transferring all stitches onto the circular needle. You can also use a darning needle but will need to use a different method for binding off and sewing the bottom of the bag.

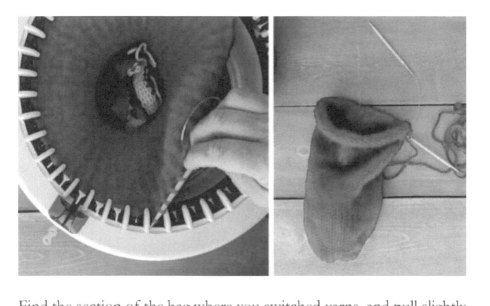

Find the section of the bag where you switched yarns, and pull slightly to straighten up the seem. Tie and trim yarn, leave about an inch on each side of the knot.

Grab your other circular knitting needle and pick up all the stitches from the lining at the bottom of the knit tube. Once all stitches from the bottom have been transferred onto the 2nd circular needle pull off waste yarn.

Grab the bottom of the tube and pull it up to meet the top of the tube, bind off.

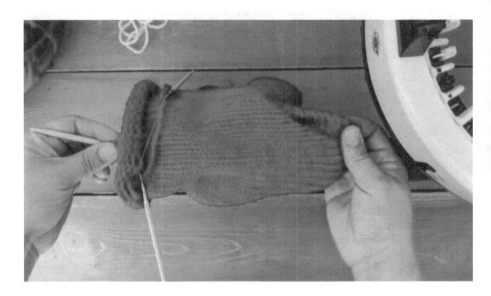

Follow the line across the bottom of the bag and stitch under the seam to close bottom of bag.

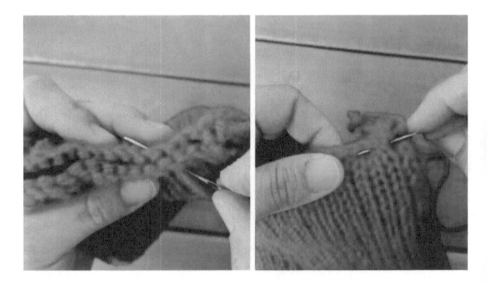

Add a ribbon to make the bag a drawstring.

Addi Boho Towel Ring

Materials:

-Addi 22 pin circular knitting machine

-26-30 yds of worsted weight yarn in main color

-5 yds of waste yarn

-Size G 4.25 mm hook

-8 or 10 mm bead or button

-2.5-3" wooden ring

-Yarn needle, scissors, measuring tape

Terms Used and Abbreviations:

Pattern is written in US terminology.

Begin(ning) - beg

Chain(s) - ch(s)

Fasten Off - FO

Repeat - Rep

Single Crochet - sc

Slip Stitch - sl st

Stitch(es) - st(s)

Yarn Over - YO

Gauge:

8 sts and 10 rows = 2" (5 cm) using medium tension for knitted portion. Gauge for crocheted portion is not imperative.

Finished Measurements:

Tube was stretched and then allowed to relax before laying flat and taking the measurements. Unfinished tube measures approx. 7.5" (19 cm) prior to assembly and not including waste yarn.

Pattern Notes:

-All cast-on and cast-off methods used in this pattern will be the provisional (basic) cast-on and cast-off methods.

-You will need to be able to read and follow basic beginner crochet pattern instructions.

-You will need to understand basic sewing techniques.

Instructions:

Towel ring is made by cinching one end of knitted tube and closing other end with sl st method. It is then crocheted to the wooden ring using basic crochet sts. A wooden bead is added for a button and the tassel (optional) is added last.

Towel Tube

1) Cast on with main color and knit 35 rows.

2) Leaving yourself a long tail for sewing and crocheting purposes later, cut yarn and add waste yarn. Knit 5 more rows.

3) Cast off.

Assembly

ZZZ1)   Beg with cast-on end and cinch shut. Thread yarn needle onto tail and reinforce your sts by taking the tail through all sts once more. Knot off but do not cut yarn.

Insert crochet hook into cast-on bottom near center and pull up a loop with leftover tail. Ch 5 (ch more if your button is larger), sl st into cast-on bottom once more to create a ch loop. This loop will be our button hole. FO and weave tail into tube.

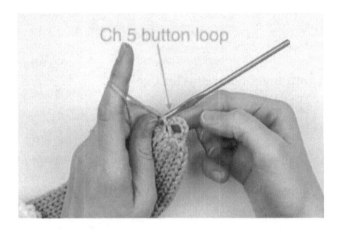

Ch 5 button loop

1)   Line sts up at cast-off end and use the sl st method to close. (Remember to leave your tail long for the next portion.) Remove waste yarn.

Insert your hook into the sl st nearest your long tail. Grab your wooden ring and attach it following these steps below.

a.   Place wooden ring between your working yarn (long tail) and your hook. Going through the wooden ring, make a sl st.

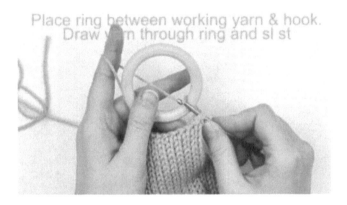

b.   Move wooden ring to the right of your work and insert your hook into 1st sl st once more. Pull up a loop (you should have 2 loops on your hook).

Move ring right, insert hook into 1st st

Pull up a loop

c.   Move ring back between your hook and working yarn. Going through the ring, YO and draw through both loops on your hook.

Move ring between hook & working yarn. Go
through ring and draw yarn through both loops

d.   Rep steps A-C in every other sl st across until you reach the end.
You should have a total of 11 sc when you are done.

Repeat process in every other st to end

e.   Sl st into piece once more and FO, weaving in your tail.

Add your bead

With a small length of yarn and your yarn needle, sew your bead onto the front of the towel ring, about mid-way down. If you are adding a tassel, be sure to leave a bit of space below the bead for the tassel to hang. Take tails to inside of tube.

Maci Beanie

Materials:

Addi Express King Size Knitting Machine

Yarn: 2 colors of Worsted Weight Yarn (1/2 ball each or 1 ball for a

solid hat)

Suggested Yarn: We Are Knitters, The Petite Wool This yarn is more of an Aran/Heavy Worsted Weight Yarn.

Yardage: 76 yards of each color or 153 yards of one color.

Waste Yarn: Waste yarn in a contrasting color to your hat.

Notions: Red Needle that comes with your Addi Machine (or bent darning needle), Pick/Hook that comes with your Addi or a bent paperclip. scissors, faux fur pom (Optional).

Circular Knitting Machine Patterns

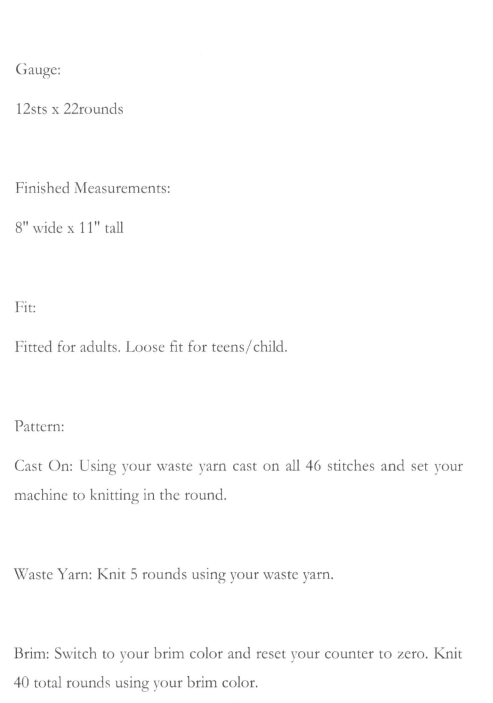

Gauge:

12sts x 22rounds

Finished Measurements:

8" wide x 11" tall

Fit:

Fitted for adults. Loose fit for teens/child.

Pattern:

Cast On: Using your waste yarn cast on all 46 stitches and set your machine to knitting in the round.

Waste Yarn: Knit 5 rounds using your waste yarn.

Brim: Switch to your brim color and reset your counter to zero. Knit 40 total rounds using your brim color.

Create Double Brim: Using your hook/pick, starting with the first brim color loop to the left of the tail next to the waste yarn. Pick up each loop and place it up on the needle. Slowly turn the handle keeping light tension on the working yarn so not to drop any stitches. Work around picking up every first stitch of the brim color and bringing it up to the needle.

Continue Brim: Still using the brim color, knit 5 more rounds.

Top Color: Switch to the top color and knit until your counter reads 70 TOTAL rounds.

Cut Waste Yarn: Cut your waste yarn off in sections and remove it from the brim. Making sure to cut only the waste yarn and not your brim color.

Cast Off: Cast off all stitches while they are still on the machine. To do so, cut your working yarn approximately 2 feet long. Thread your working yarn onto the red needle that came with your Addi or a bent darning needle. Turning your machine slowly, place your needle under each stitch as you come to them and thread the needle through each stitch. Thread the yarn through all of the stitches and pull tight to close. Sew the remaining yarn through the top of your hat a few times to close.

Finishing: Weave in ends, block and attach a pom if you like!

Colorful Twist Headband

Materials:

Addi Express King Size Knitting Machine

Yarn: 2 colors of Fingering Weight Yarn (1/3 ball (133 yards) each or

Circular Knitting Machine Patterns

1 ball (133 yards) of worsted weight yarn for a solid headband)

Suggested Yarn: Knit Picks – Hawthorne Speckle Handpainted, Knit Picks – Muse Hand Painted Sock Yarn, Knit Picks – Stroll Hand Painted. (Or some of your favorite indie dyed yarn)

Yardage: 76 yards of each color or 153 yards of one color.

Waste Yarn: Waste yarn in a contrasting color.

Notions: Scissors, 4.00mm Crochet Hook, Tapestry Needle.

Gauge:

12sts x 22rounds

Finished Measurements:

8" wide x 6" tall – after seaming

Fit:

Fitted for adults. Loose fit for teens/child.

Pattern:

Cast On: Using your waste yarn cast on all 46 stitches and set your machine to knitting in the round.

Waste Yarn: Knit 5-7 rounds using your waste yarn.

Headband: Switch to your headband colors. Leaving a 2 foot tail for seaming and holding both strands of fingering weight yarns at the same time begin knitting with your main colors. Remember to reset your counter to zero. Knit 77 total rounds using your headband colors.

Waste Yarn: Break your main color yarns leaving a 10" tail and put your waste yarn back onto your machine. Knit 5-7 rounds using your waste yarn.

Cast Off: Cast off all stitches by simply turning your machine and letting the stitches fall off the needles.

Closing Up the Ends: Close each end using your crochet hook and starting at the side opposite your tail. Place your crochet hook through the first stitch of the main color and the stitch that's furthest away from the tail. Pull the first stitch to the right of that loop through the first loop. Go across to the left side and grab that first stitch and pull it through the current stitch on your hook. To see this in detail please see min 11:50 of the video tutorial. Continue down the side grabbing the next stitch/loop and pulling it through the current stitch on your hook. Once you have reached the end where your tail is pull the tail through your final stitch to secure and close it up.

Now pull off the waste yarn for that side by unraveling it or cutting it and pulling it out. Being careful not to cut the main headband.

Repeat this closure for the other end of the headband.

Seaming: Lay your headband flat on the table. Take one end and turn it over 180 degrees to create a twist in the middle of the headband. Now bring both ends together in the middle. Seam these ends together using the mattress stitch. See min 20:00 in the video tutorial for additional details.

Finishing: Weave ends in between both sides of the headband through the seam to secure.

DIY Rainbow Wall Hanging

Materials:

22 Pin Knitting Machine

Worsted Weight Yarn – you will need 7 colors plus a large skein of white for the pom poms

*Suggested Yarns:

Hand Made Modern available at Target

Red Heart Super Saver available on Amazon

Mainstays Basic Yarn available at Walmart

Premier Just Worsted

5 EVA Foam Dowels 15 mm x 24 inches

Darning Needle

Pom Pom Maker

*Other yarns can be used, however tension and rows may vary depending on the type of yarn you choose.

The sizes that you need for each piece of the rainbow are:

Red – 24 inches

Orange – 21 inches

Yellow – 18.5 inches

Green 15.5 inches

Blue – 12.5 inches

Indigo – 9.5 inches

Violet – 6 inches

Knitting The Tubes

When knitting your tubes, cast on as you normally would with each color but leave a long yarn tail for each, at least 40" for the tail that you cast on with, that way you will have plenty of yarn to use when sewing the tubes together. The smaller tubes you can leave less than 40" for the tail.

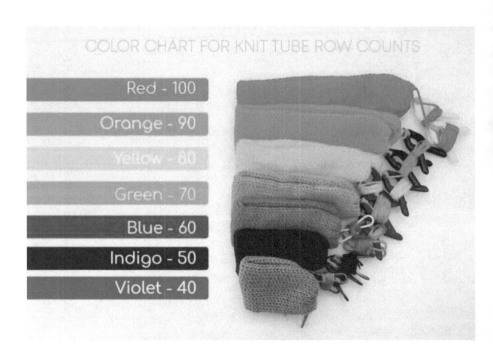

Crank out the number of rows for each color listed below for a 7 color rainbow

Red – 100

Orange – 90

Yellow – 80

Green 70

Blue – 60

Indigo – 50

Violet – 40

If you want to make less arches in your rainbow, start with 40 rows then add 10 rows for each color. Be sure to cut the right size dowel, if you use 40 rounds to start, and end with your last tube with 80 rows for a 5 color rainbow, cut the size tube for each color on the chart, you can choose whatever color you want for your actual tubes.

Putting the Rainbow Together

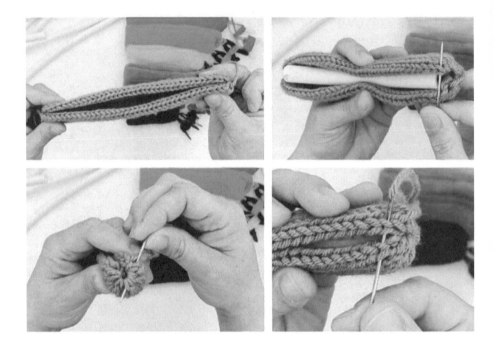

Fold your tube in half like a hot dog bun and place foam dowel inside. Starting with the long yarn tail with your darning needle stitch the end closed then sew along the edge to the other end and stitch closed. Tie the yarn tails and cut one tail off so that you just have one yarn tail (the longest one) remaining. Repeat for all colors.

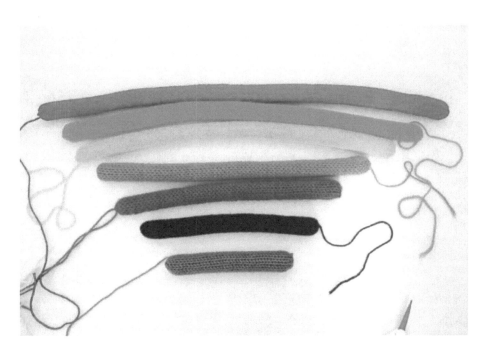

In the above image the yarn tails alternate on each side. The red, yellow, blue and violet tails are on the left and the orange, green and indigo are on the right. This helps when sewing the arches together.

Once you have all of your tubes sewn around the foam dowel and the extra yarn tail trimmed off lay your tubes out in the order of the rainbow with the smallest size on the bottom. Alternate the yarn tail ends so that not all of the yarn tails are on the same side.

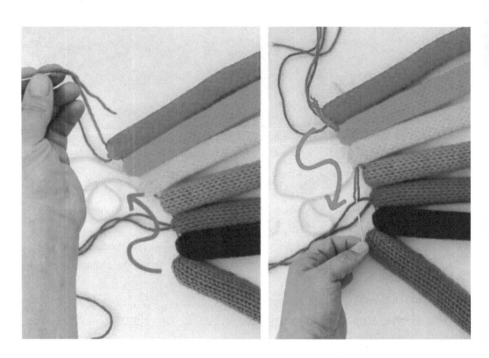

Starting with the violet yarn tail, thread the yarn through the ends of each tube up to the top. Then grab the red tail and thread through each tube bringing it down to the bottom. Repeat with the other color tails so that half are at the top and half are at the bottom.

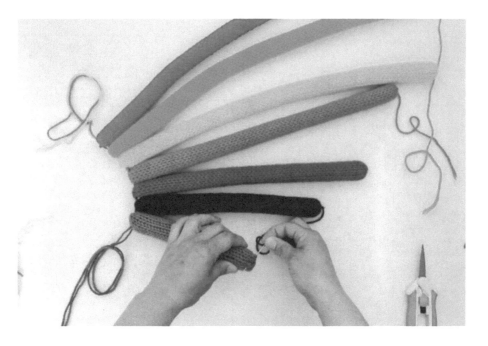

Repeat for the opposite side. Be sure to bring the indigo yarn tail down through the violet tube first before going back up to the top of the red tube. Do the same with the Orange tail bringing it up through the red tube end before bringing it down to the bottom.

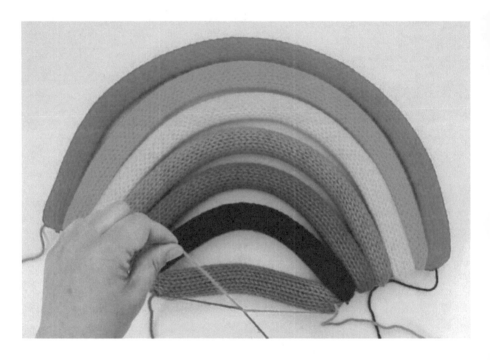

Once you have all of the yarn tails sewn through the tubes tie 2 of the tails tight on the bottom. This will create the arch of the rainbow. tie the bottom closed with the top to color yarn.

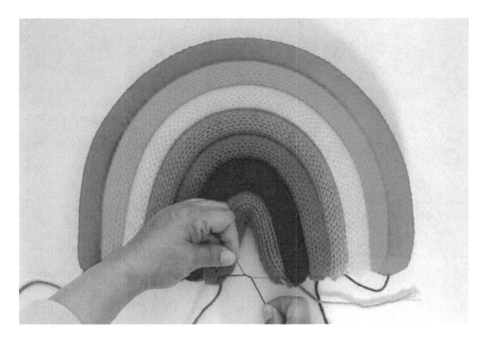

Be sure not to tie too tight, you want an opening at the bottom.

Flip the rainbow to the back side. Take all of the remaining yarn tails and sew the arches together by bringing the yarn up under the yarn on the tubes. sort of zig zag as shown in the image below.

Add a loop by threading yarn up along each of the tubes. Start at the bottom center of the rainbow and come up through the top. Loop the yarn and tie a knot around one of the stitches on the top. Then bring the yarn back down to the bottom and tie together with the other yarn tail. Cut yarn and weave in ends.

Now make your pom poms.

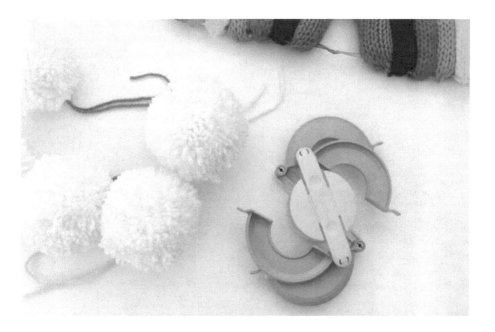

After you have all 6 of your pom poms made you can tie them on.

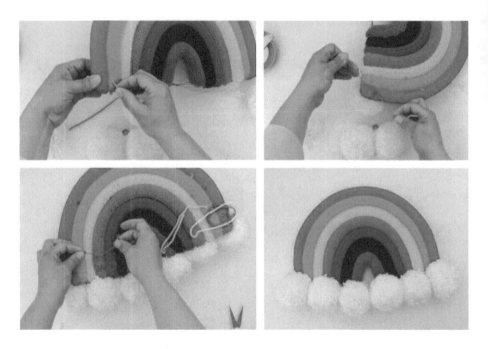

Weave the yarn tail up a bit on the back of the tube, tie off and cut yarn.

Jellyfish

Materials:

22 Pin Knitting Machine

Worsted Weight Size 4 Yarn

Suggested yarns

Loops & Threads Coastal Cotton

Yarn Bee Lil'Dollop

Premier Yarn Just Worsted – purchased at the Dollar Tree but other acrylic worsted weight yarns will do fine.

H8 5.0 mm Crochet Hook

Poly-fil

Safety Eyes or Buttons

Darning Needle

Scissors

Tension: Moderate

Finished Measurements: Jellyfish head only, tentacles will vary depending on style.

Small: 2.5" x 2.5"

Large: 3" x 2.5"

Tension used will determine the amount of stretch and overall size of finished jellyfish as well as the type of yarn used and how much stuffing you put in.

Using different yarns other than the suggested yarns result in the size of the jellyfish being different but any worsted weight yarn that works on your machine should be fine.

Small Jellyfish – Crank 30 rows for jellyfish head

Large Jellyfish – Crank 40 rows for jellyfish head

Making your little jellyfish's head

Once you have your tube knit, fold it inside itself and cinch one end closed.

Flip the tube inside out so that your yarn tails are now on the inside, tie in a few knots. Trim the yarn tails so they are about 2.5" or so. Thread a piece of yarn or use one of the pieces of yarn cut off from the yarn tails (if it is long enough) onto your darning needle and pick up every other stitch along the folded edge. You will be creating a drawstring to cinch the tube closed.

Adding the safety eyes

Stuff the tube with Poly-fil and and then cinch slightly to close. Place the safety eyes where you want them, then take out the Poly-fil.

Secure the safety eyes in place then re-stuff the poly-fil and cinch closed.

Thread your drawstring through all the loops once more and cinch closed. Tie a knot and hide your yarn tails under some stitches before cutting off.

Frill

slst around a single ring of knit stitches on the bottom of the jellyfish head, slst to join stitches. Start at the opposite side of the eyes.

ch2, 2 hdc into 1st slst. slst into the next st. *3 hdc into the next st, slst into the next st. Repeat from * until you reach the beginning.

In the first st where you did the 2 hdc, do 1 hdc over the ch2, join with a slst.

The Tentacles

Terms: in US terms

ch = Chain

hdc = Half Double Crochet

sc = Single Crochet

slst = Slip Stitch

Listed below are the tentacles, pick 2 or 3 tentacle styles and work an even number (6 or 8 depending on which size jellyfish you are making or whatever you feel like)

When you crochet your tentacles they will be very curly like a corkscrew, if you pull on them slightly they will elongate.

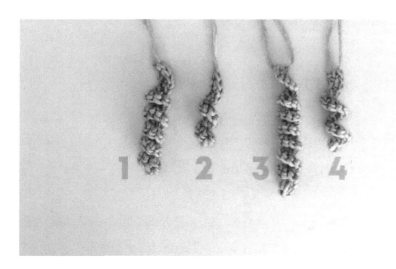

Tentacle 1:

Chain 17, 4 hdc into the 2nd chain from your hook. 3 sc into each chain across until the last st, 1 sc in the last st.

Tentacle 2:

Chain 11, 2 hdc into the 2nd chain from your hook. 2 sc into each chain across until the last st, 1 sc in the last st.

Tentacle 3:

Chain 23, 4 hdc into the 2nd chain from your hook. 3 sc into each chain across until the last st 1 sc in the last st.

Tentacle 4:

Chain 13, 2 hdc into the 2nd chain from your hook. 1 sc into each chain across until the last st, 1 sc in the last st.

Tentacle Pattern: Sample is worked using Tentacles 2 & 3

Step 1: Chain 11, 2 hdc into the 2nd chain from your hook. 2 sc into each chain across until the last st, 1 sc into the last st.

Step 2: Chain 23, 4 hdc into the 2nd chain from your hook. 3 sc into each chain across until the last st, 1 sc into the last st.

Repeat Steps 1 and 2 three more times so that you have a total of 8 tentacles for the large jellyfish, or repeat two more times for a total of 6 tentacles for the small jellyfish.

Form tentacles into a ring and join with a slip stitch, make sure your stitches aren't twisted.

Sc evenly across and join with a slst.

Turn the jellyfish head upside down and lay the tentacle ring on top.

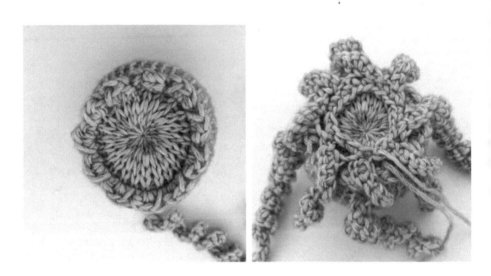

Using one of the yarn tails from the tentacles, stitch the tentacles to the bottom of the jellyfish head using the top of the single crochet stitches as your guide.

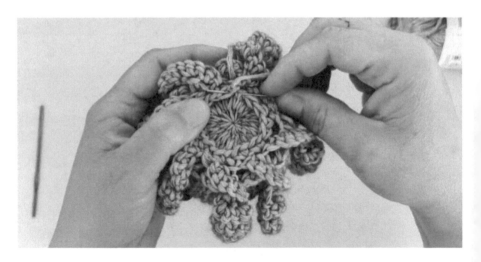

When you get back to your starting point tie yarn tails together. At this point you can hide the yarn tails and cut off and you are finished with your little jellyfish.

These little jellyfish can be given as a little gift or made into a mobile.

Made in United States
Troutdale, OR
09/21/2024

23028481R00037